sentatives: General Publishing Co., Ltd.,
Don Mills, Ontario M3B 2T6.

t indicates the number of this printing.

ess Cataloging-in-Publication Number 94–67588

46–8

or photographs by Jim Graham
or design by Nancy Loggins Gonzalez
Borgenicht
rs Condensed by Deborah Lugar

e ordered by mail from the publisher.
0 for postage and handling.
kstore first!

Book Publishers
ty-second Street
nnsylvania 19103–4399

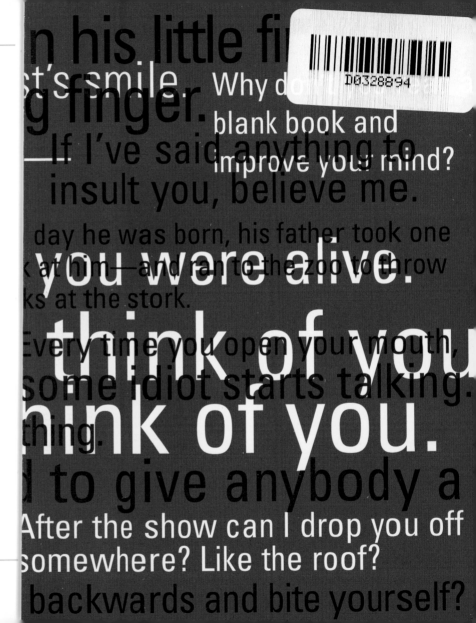

HI
YOU

BI(
IN

MORE TH
AND
FROM THE

Canadian rep
30 Lesmill Ro

9 8 7 6 5 4 3 2
Digit on the r

Library of Cor

ISBN 1–56138

Cover and inte
Cover and inte
Edited by Dav
Typeset in Uni

This book may
Please add $2
But try your b

Running Press
125 South Twe
Philadelphia, I

Contents

Introduction. 4

"Don't move—I want to forget you just the way you are,"
and Other General Insults 7

CHAPTER TWO

"Why don't you go to a window and lean out too far?"
and Other Insulting Suggestions 31

"What would you charge to sour a quart of milk?"
and Other Remarks About Looks 39

CHAPTER FOUR

"You make silence a wonderful thing to look forward to,"
and Other Remarks About Speech. 65

"Can I use your head for my rock garden?"
and Other Intelligent Comments 73

"Next time you cook with gas, inhale some,"
and Other Harmful Wishes 87

CHAPTER SEVEN

"You light up a room when you leave it,"
and Other Personal Attacks 95

"You'd make a perfect stranger,"
and Other Parting Thoughts 119

Introduction

In the 1920s, at the Swan Lake Inn in the Catskill Mountains of upstate New York, I was a *tummeler*. In Yiddish, this word means "noisemaker." And that was basically my job description. My charge was to keep people busy and happy, and not let them think about how crummy the food or the rooms were at the resort.

The *tummeler* is part of a proud Jewish tradition that dates back to the Middle Ages. Back then there was a guy named a *badchen* whose job it was to run around at weddings, make lots of slapstick noise and do whatever was necessary to keep everybody giggling.

At the Swan Lake Inn, doing "whatever was necessary" meant a *tummeler* also had to be an emcee, a scenic designer, an electrician, and sometimes even a busboy. And the main currency for all these jobs was the one-liner.

If a guest complained about the size of his room, for instance, I'd say, "My room's so small,

the mice are hunchbacks."

Or if they'd heard that one, I'd try, **"You should see my room. I put the key in the door and it breaks the window.** When I complained, they gave me a room without a window."

Complaints, I found, often led to the best one-liners. In fact, I was present at the invention of one of the most famous one-liners of all time. Unfortunately, I didn't make this joke up—it came my way from an angry older Jewish woman complaining to me about the fare at the inn.

"The food here is terrible," she said to me. "And such small portions!"

A classic. In reply, I simply said, **"Madam, the food at the Swan Lake Inn is fit for a king. Here, King! Here, King!"**

That was the point of *tummeling*—to make a quick hit with a funny line or gag, then get out of the way quickly.

My love of insults and one-liners came from this mountain laboratory. You had to be able to rat-a-tat-tat them out, on all subjects, to all kinds of people, every hour, day or night.

For some reason, a lot of our guests liked to be insulted—albeit gently.

"I'd like to say we're glad you're here," I'd tell a guy. "I'd like to say it."

Or, "The last time I saw you, you were in a nightmare."

Or seeing a couple arguing in the lobby, I might break the tension by saying, "Here's a fastidious couple. She's fast, and he's hideous."

Maybe you had to be there. But it seemed to do the job, and they seemed to love it at the time.

I hope you will, too.

Henny Youngman

CHAPTER ONE

"DON'T MOVE —I WANT TO FORGET YOU JUST THE WAY YOU ARE,"

AND OTHER GENERAL INSULTS

It's good to see you. It means you're not behind my back.

For a minute I didn't recognize you. It was the most enjoyable minute I ever spent.

Here's what happens when two first cousins get married.

Here's a guy who could make his wife a lucky widow.

At least he gives his wife something to live for: **a divorce.**

You remind me of something I want to forget.

You've always been a big help to people. But so has Ex-Lax.

You want to be remembered . . . by anyone!

I'd like to introduce you to some friends of mine—I want to break off with them.

If you ever need a friend—buy a dog.

Is your family happy, or do you go home at night?

He always gets the last word in a family argument:

"Yes, dear."

What do you do for a living? You are living, aren't you?

He's so old that he remembers when toothpaste was white.

He's so old that when they lit the candles on his last birthday cake the smoke alarm went off.

He has music even his shoes

You have the Midas touch. Everything you touch turns to a muffler.

He has more talent in his little finger—than he has in his big finger.

in his soul— squeak.

He is so full of alcohol that if anyone gives him a hot-foot he'll burn for three days.

I wish I had known you when you were alive.

You only have one bad habit— breathing!

He willed his body to science. Science is contesting the will.

Maybe you'd be okay once I got to know you—but I don't want to take a chance.

I never met a man I didn't like—until I met you.

When I go to Israel, I'll have a tree uprooted in your honor.

With 50,000 manholes in this city, you had to drop in here!

I'm sorry to announce that we have two disappointments tonight. Robert Redford couldn't make it, and she could.

As a failure, you are a fantastic success.

She was chosen Miss America when she was sixteen. Of course, there were very few Americans in those days.

If they can make penicillin out of moldy bread, surely they can make something out of you.

Please call me some day so I can hang up on you.

I hear you're getting a divorce—who's the lucky woman?

Very few people know this man was born an only twin.

There's nothing wrong with you that a miracle won't cure.

Don't tell me—I know who you are. You're the reason for birth control!

If there's ever a price on your head, take it!

Waiting for you to make it big
is like leaving
a light on for
Jimmy Hoffa.

You couldn't make the winners laugh in
Las Vegas.

The only place you could make a name for yourself is a hotel register.

The more I think of you the less I think of you.

I need you like Venice needs a street-sprinkler.

With the cost of living so high, **why bother?**

Does your Parole Board know you're up this late?

Stick around while I have a few drinks—it'll make you witty.

I love the decor in your house: it looks like early Salvation Army.

If you ever need a friend—I'll go find one.

When he's sick he goes to stores and reads the get-well cards.

His only friend is his ex-wife's attorney.

You're perfect for hot weather—
you leave me cold.

He doesn't have an enemy in the world—he's outlived them all.

You're as phony as a dentist's smile.

You remind me of shampoo— always getting in everyone's hair.

You made a big mistake today. You got out of bed.

You make me as happy as an un-tipped waiter.

Do tell me all about yourself. I adore horror stories.

You may be down to earth—but not down far enough to suit me.

If you were alive, you'd be a very sick man.

Here's the perfect example of what happens if you take an overdose of Geritol.

· "DON'T MOVE—I WANT TO FORGET YOU JUST THE WAY YOU ARE,"

You're one of the main reasons for twin beds.

When you get back home, give my regards to the warden.

If you have your life to live over again—don't do it.

I don't believe in reincarnation, **but what were you when you were alive?**

I'm going to name my first ulcer after you.

He's like buried treasure. Too bad they dug him up.

I've known this man through thick and thick.

I think the world of you—
and you know what shape the world is in.

I like you.
I have no taste,
but I like you.

There's only one thing wrong with you. You're visible.

You're not entirely useless— you can be used as a bad example.

Don't move—I want to forget you just the way you are.

"WHY DON'T YOU GO TO A WINDOW AND **LEAN** OUT **TOO FAR?**"

AND OTHER INSULTING SUGGESTIONS

Why don't you buy a house and stay there?

Why don't you go on a diet and quit eating my heart out?

Why don't you ask your undertaker for an estimate?

Why don't you read a blank book **and improve your mind?**

Why don't you go home—your cage must be cleaned out by now?

Why don't you put your teeth in backwards and bite yourself?

Why don't you start neglecting your appearance? Maybe it'll go away.

Why don't you go and get lost somewhere where they have no "found" department?

Why don't you take a vacation—say, for about ten years?

Why don't you stick your head out the window—feet first?

Why don't you sit down and rest your brains?

Why don't you send your wits out to be sharpened?

Why don't you go to a window and lean out too far?

Why don't you step outside for a few years?

Why don't you freeze your teeth and give your tongue a sleigh ride?

Why don't you make your wife happy and run away?

Why don't you resign from the human race?

Why don't you crawl back under your rock?

Why don't you pawn yourself and lose the ticket?

Why don't you buy a jar of vanishing cream
and use it?

Why don't you sue your brains for non-support?

Why don't you shrink your head and use it as a paperweight?

Why don't you put your glasses on backwards and walk into yourself?

CHAPTER THREE

"WHAT WOULD YOU CHARGE TO SOUR A QUART OF MILK?"

AND OTHER REMARKS ABOUT LOOKS

If Moses had seen you, there'd be another Commandment.

She has Early American features—she looks
like a buffalo.

There's a guy who lives alone and looks it.

You're as pretty as a picture—and you should be hung.

He's not listed in *Who's Who,* he's in *What's That.*

She would look perfect in something long and flowing—say, a river.

Here's a fastidious couple. He's fast and she's hideous!

You look like a side dish that nobody ordered.

Do you have a chip on your shoulder, or is that your head?

People like you don't just grow on trees—they swing from them.

O.K., you've seen your shadow. Now crawl back into your hole.

Didn't I see you once before—under a microscope?

If you were a building, you'd be condemned.

I heard you were at the dog show. Who won *second* prize?

Someone should press the down button on his

elevator shoes.

You look like you got your hair cut in a pet shop.

Barbers don't charge him for cutting his hair—they charge for searching for it!

You should really let your hair grow—right down over your face.

Is that your hair, or did you just walk through a car wash?

Is that your face, or is it Halloween?

He has a suit for every day of the month—the one he has on.

That's a lovely dress you have—
who shot the couch?

That's a nice suit you're wearing. When did the clown die?

Who gave you that tie? Somebody angry with you?

Was that suit made to order? The guy didn't pick it up, huh?

He has an interesting hobby—he collects old clothes and wears them.

I like the suit you're wearing.
Who shines it for you?

I love that jacket you're wearing. It's obvious you shop at only the finest garage sales.

I'm not saying he's a square—but they built a town around him.

Your tailor must have had a good sense of humor.

Hey, I love your suit. K-Mart, right?

I like that outfit you're wearing. You should hang on to it—it'll come back in style some day.

I love that suit you're wearing. You never throw anything away, do you?

He looks like he dressed in front of an airplane propeller.

He dresses like an unmade bed.

His clothes came back from the laundry—they refused to accept them.

His suits all have that Italian look—wine stains down the front.

I'm glad to see you— I didn't even know the circus was in town.

She's a brunette by nature—**but a blonde by Clairol.**

What happened—did an undertaker do an incomplete job on you?

I hear the President is going to declare you a national disaster area.

I know an organization that would like to help you— **the ASPCA.**

What is that you have on—your face?

You look just as bad as your passport photo.

There's only one thing wrong with your face— **it's on the outside.**

She has a figure like a leopard. Good in spots.

He sent his photo to the lonely-hearts club. They sent it back and said, **"We're not *that* lonely!"**

Your face is familiar—I just can't recall the museum.

As an outsider, what do you think of the human race?

Your face has more wrinkles than an accordion.

She looks like a million bucks—green and wrinkled.

She has bedroom eyes—a pillow under each one.

The last time I saw a mouth like yours there was a fish-hook in it.

Have you ever been to the zoo? I mean, as a visitor?

You know, there's one good thing about your body: it's not as ugly as your face.

You're certainly shipshape— shaped like a ship.

He's so bow-legged he has to have his trousers pressed in a circle.

The last time I saw you, you were in my nightmare.

You know, I never thought I'd see anything that looks like you without digging.

You're so repulsive, even a boomerang wouldn't come back to you.

Excuse me while I go out for a cup of coffee. I have to steady my nerves before I take another look at you.

When you get up in the morning, who puts you together?

Your face looks like you slept in it.

Four drunks looked at him—they took the pledge.

You look like something that has been stuffed by a good taxidermist.

You still look like you did twenty years ago—bad!

She's the kind of girl you take to the movies **when you want to see the picture.**

You have a lot of funny lines—too bad they're all in your face.

Look at you—was anyone else hurt in the accident?

You look as though you're doing time just by living.

You look like a talent scout for a cemetery.

How much would you charge to haunt a house?

If looks could kill, you'd be forced to wear a mask.

I'd put a curse on you, but somebody beat me to it.

Your features don't seem to know the importance of teamwork.

She's got her good looks from her father— **he's a plastic surgeon.**

She doesn't need a plastic surgeon—
she needs a wrecking crew.

Did you have your face lifted or your body lowered?

When I look at your face, I wonder what Mother Nature had in mind.

Don't you love nature—despite what it did to you?

Sit down—you make the place look shabby.

Would you mind looking at me?
I've got the hiccups.

I never forget a face—but in your case I'll make an exception.

Did anyone ever tell you you were beautiful, and mean it?

What would you charge to sour a quart of milk?

When you were born, did the doctor know **which end to slap?**

He was born at home, but when his mother saw him she went to the hospital.

The day he was born, his father took one look at him—and ran to the zoo to throw rocks at the stork.

He's so ugly that when he was born the doctor slapped his mother.

If I had a face like yours, I'd sue my parents.

Be it ever so homely, there's no face like yours.

When I first spotted you I thought my eyes were bad—now I wish they were.

Was the ground cold when you crawled out this morning?

I can't forget the first time I laid eyes on you—
and don't think I haven't tried.

"YOU MAKE SILENCE A WONDERFUL THING TO LOOK FORWARD TO,"

AND OTHER REMARKS ABOUT SPEECH

You have a fine voice—why spoil it by talking?

You're like a slow leak—people hear you but they can't turn you off.

She has a black belt in mouth.

He is the only person who enters the room mouth first.

It's always difficult to follow an outstanding speaker. Fortunately, I don't have that problem tonight.

If he ever had to eat his words, he'd put on
fifteen pounds.

I wish you were on TV—so I could turn you off.

You should be wired for silence.

He has such a big mouth he can eat a banana sideways.

Please close your mouth
so I can see who you are.

You remind me of a clarinet—a wind instrument.

Your mouth is getting too big for your muzzle.

If you ever bite your tongue, you'll die from acid poisoning.

I can always tell when you're lying—
your lips are moving.

If you'll stop telling lies about me,
I'll stop telling the truth about you.

Every time you open your mouth, **some idiot starts talking.**

I'm not hard of hearing, I'm just ignoring you.

I understand everything—except what you're saying.

If you think of something to say, don't mention it.

I wish I had a hearing aid so I could turn you off.

If you have something to say,

shut up.

Is your speech over, or can I finish my nap?

You make silence a wonderful thing to look forward to.

CHAPTER FIVE

"CAN I USE YOUR HEAD FOR MY ROCK GARDEN?"

AND OTHER INTELLIGENT COMMENTS

You have a wonderful head on your shoulders—
whose is it?

I enjoyed talking to you—my mind needed a rest.

He has a one-track mind—with one rail missing.

Can I use your head for my rock garden?

He's nobody's fool—**he's a freelancer.**

He has an open mind—and it should be closed for repairs.

He used to go to school with his dog. But one day they were separated—his dog graduated.

He has a mind that reminds me of an auction . . .
going, going, gone.

She reminds me of a bottle of beer. Both are empty from the neck up.

You sure have a great mind—too bad it never reached your head.

What does your brain want to be when it grows up?

Next time you order a
toupee, get one with
a brain.

You have a great
mind—why don't you
use it sometime?

Are you
always so
stupid, or is
today a
special
occasion?

Are you naturally
stupid, or did a terrorist
hijack your brain?

You should go to a dentist and have some wisdom teeth put in.

Can you really afford to give anybody a piece of your mind?

It takes real talent to be as dumb as you are.

I don't know what makes you so stupid, **but it really works.**

You appear to be as happy as if you were in your right mind.

Are you naturally stupid or are you waiting for a brain transplant?

I know you're not as stupid as you look. Nobody could be.

What's the latest dope—besides you?

He thinks of himself as a wit. He's only half right.

He was born April 2—a day too late.

You got an idea? Beginner's luck!

Every time he gets into a taxi, the driver keeps the "vacant" sign lit.

Keep talking—someday you'll say something intelligent.

You could be the perfect understudy **for an idiot.**

As a conductor, he doesn't know his brass from his oboe.

Here's a group that actually made a record. The only reason it didn't sell is that they forgot to put a hole in the middle.

If it weren't for your stupidity, you'd have no personality at all.

What's on your mind? If you'll forgive the overstatement.

If there's an idea in your head, it's in solitary confinement.

He once said, and I quote, "Of all the things I've lost, I miss my mind the most."

How much of a refund do you expect to get on that head, **now that it's empty?**

Please don't come any closer. I'm allergic to ignorance.

You have a keen sense of stupidity.

Look, I'm not going to engage in a battle of wits with you—I refuse to attack an unarmed man.

In your case, brain surgery would only be a minor operation.

If you had a brain transplant, the brain would reject you.

You could be brainwashed with an eyedropper.

Your mind is as sharp as a marble.

Anyone who offered you a penny for your thoughts **would be over-paying.**

His mind is like a steel trap—always closed.

I've got two minutes to kill— **so tell me all you know.**

I bet you're called a big thinker by people who lisp.

He's a little slow. It takes him an hour and a half to watch *60 Minutes*.

I'm paid to make an idiot of myself. Why do you do it for free?

"NEXT TIME YOU COOK WITH GAS, INHALE SOME,"

AND OTHER HARMFUL WISHES

I understand you throw yourself into everything you do. **Why don't you go dig a deep well?**

Next time you cook with gas, inhale some.

Do me a favor—on your way home make it a point to jaywalk.

There's only one thing that keeps me from breaking you in half—I don't want two of you around.

I'd like to run into you again—sometime when **I'm driving and you're walking.**

He called the suicide hotline and they said, "You're doing the right thing."

The last time he was in the hospital, he got get-well cards from all the nurses.

People owe a lot to him—ulcers, nausea, diarrhea.

You know, I'd like to send you a Valentine, but I haven't figured out how to wrap lace around a time bomb.

If I've said anything to offend you, I meant it.

If there's never been a suicide in your family, why don't you break the monotony?

If I've said anything to insult you, believe me.

If I have offended you, I'll gladly repeat it.

I wish somebody would kidnap you, but who would they contact?

I don't know what makes you tick, but I hope it's a time bomb.

After the show off somewhere?

can I drop you Like the roof?

There's a train leaving in an hour—
be under it!

"YOU LIGHT UP A
ROOM WHEN
YOU
LEAVE IT,"

AND OTHER PERSONAL ATTACKS

You don't seem to be yourself lately—and I've noticed the improvement.

I never forget a face, and in your case I'll remember both of them.

I know you have to be somebody,
but why do you have to be you?

Someday you'll find yourself, and will you be disappointed!

He has that certain nothing.

I'm planning to invite you to my party—there's always room for one bore.

The party's over—you just arrived.

You have a knack for making strangers immediately.

The things he does for his friends can be counted on one little finger.

You may not have any enemies, but none of your friends like you.

I'd like to introduce you to a man with no equals—only superiors.

Much has been written and said about him and he is here tonight to deny it.

He thinks he's quite a big wheel.
Of course, you know what dogs do to wheels.

You're the kind of person that makes coffee nervous.

He doesn't get ulcers, he gives them.

You remind me of a chocolate bar—you're half nuts.

This guy is tighter than the top olive in a bottle.

You can always recognize him in a restaurant. He's the one sitting with his back to the check.

He has more crust than a pie factory.

There's a pair of shoes with three heels.

His friends don't know what to get him for Christmas. What do you get for a guy who's had everybody?

Even his car is shiftless.

He's so full of bull that cows follow him home.

He only goes out with girls who wear glasses— he breathes on the lenses so they can't see what he's doing.

He comes from a rich family—his brother is worth $50,000 dead or alive.

He has property in Las Vegas. Caesar's Palace is holding his luggage.

He should have been an undertaker—he has no use for anyone living.

He's hoping for a lucky stroke—**his rich uncle's.**

He's so cheap, even his 8 x 10 photos are 7 x 9.

He's so stingy, you'd think he was saving money for a rainy century.

He's so cheap, he went on his honeymoon alone.

He asked for separate checks at the wedding.

You have as much of a future as an ice cube.

He's not afraid of work—he's fought it for years and won!

He does a real bang-up job in his work. He's a garbage collector.

The band leader comes from a family with a turn for music. They were organ grinders.

Our next entertainer needs no introduction—
he needs an act.

Next we have an act that is rapidly becoming an institution, which is where it belongs.

Now the band that inspired that great saying—"Stop the music!"

When they heard she was being honored tonight, everybody shouted, **"WHY?"**

He has a lot of degrees—a B.A., an M.A., a Ph.D.—but no J.O.B.

Let me tell you about our guest of honor—never has a man been more sworn at, more spit upon, more maligned . . . and rightfully so!

His career has had more **ups** and **downs**
than a bed in a honeymoon suite.

He also does magic. Last night he disappeared with the host's wife.

He always does an honest day's work—of course, it usually takes him a week to do it.

He's so lazy they named a shoe after him—
the loafer.

He is such a loser, he gives failure a bad name.

He left his job due to illness—his boss got sick and tired of him.

You're the kind of person I'd like to have over when I have the measles.

He has such a split personality that his towels are marked "His" and "His."

You could be a nurse—you like giving people the needle.

He has a personality like an army blanket.

She is as cold as a mother-in-law's kiss.

I bet you're the type who goes to libraries just to tear the last chapter out of mystery novels.

He was the only kid I knew who was abandoned by the orphanage.

Did your parents ever ask you to run away from home?

I think your family tree needs trimming.

Some people bring happiness wherever they go. You bring happiness *whenever* you go.

When she was young, someone gave her bad advice—they said, "Be yourself."

Don't you ever get tired of having yourself around?

He's a legend in his own mind.

Why did you give up your charm school lessons so early?

He's a real pain in the neck—of course, some people have a lower opinion of him.

Your manners aren't half bad— **they're all bad!**

You have an even disposition—miserable all the time.

Your presence makes me long for your absence.

If you want to be different, why don't you act normal?

He has an unlisted personality.

You light up a room when you leave it.

He's the kind of guy who throws Mexican jumping beans to the pigeons.

I remember you—you're a graduate of the Don Rickles Charm School.

You're as welcome as a phone call during a

World Series game.

If you ever get really lucky you may be elected an honorary human being.

Some people are has-beens. You are a never-was.

It's obvious you've had a charisma bypass.

What you need is a personality transplant.

You have a nice but not for a

I'd like to see you act like a human being—
but I know you don't do imitations.

You could be arrested for impersonating a human being.

How did you get out? Did someone leave your cage open?

personality—human being.

His life is so dull he can actually write his diary one week in advance.

You can write the story of her life on a piece of confetti.

Stay with me—I want to be alone.

His life is so dull, he looks forward to dental appointments.

Her idea of a hot evening is turning up the thermostat.

CHAPTER EIGHT

"YOU'D MAKE A PERFECT STRANGER,"

AND OTHER PARTING THOUGHTS

May we have the pleasure of your absence?

A day away from you is like a month in the country.

I'd like to help you out— which way did you come in?

As guests go, I wish you would.

If you have your life to live over again—
do it overseas.

Well, things could be worse—you could be here in person.

If you lend him money, you'll never see him again. And it's worth it!

Too bad you're not lost.
I could turn you in for the reward.

I admit that you're a distant relative—trouble is,
you're not distant enough.

Don't these nice sunny days make you wish you were alive?

On his first day at his new sales job, he got two orders: **"Get out!"** and **"Stay out!"**

Let's go someplace where we can each be alone.

I like long walks— take one?

I'd like to take back my introduction to you.

If I gave you a fine send-off, would you go away?

Someday you'll go too far—and I hope you stay there.

why don't you

It's nice hearing from you—next time, send a postcard.

After not seeing you for so long, all I want to say is, **"So long."**

Anything goes tonight,
and you may be
the first.

It was nice of you to come. When are
you going?

If you have anything else to do tonight—don't
neglect it!

I can't think of what I'd do
without you—but I'd rather.

I can't think of what I'd do without you—but it's worth a try.

You'd make a perfect stranger.

Next time you give your clothes away, stay in them.

Next time you pass my house, I'll appreciate it.

as more talent
as phony as a den
he has in his
s a one-track min
he rail missing.
ou crawl back under
ad known you whe
You light up a room when you leave it.
us you've had
ma bypass.
loss I
has that certain
really affe
ir of shoes wit
your mind
put your teet

If you ever need me, **please hesitate to call.**

I'll never forget the first time we met—but I'm trying.

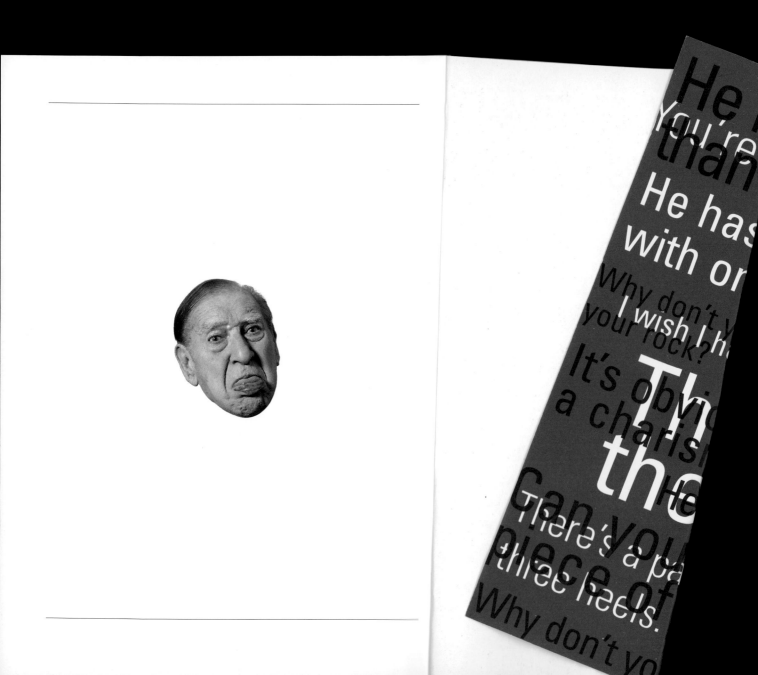